KEY TO THE COVENANT

KEY TO THE COVENANT

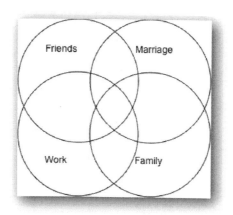

Joel Fine, M.D.

Previously by Dr. Fine
Arc of the Covenant

ISBN-13: 9781533415219
ISBN-10: 1533415218

CONTENTS

Introduction · vii

Chapter 1   All Couples Are Equal · · · · · · · · · · · · · · · · · 1
Chapter 2   Everything Has a Process and a Content · · · · 7
Chapter 3   Everything Anybody Ever Does Makes
            Sense to Them · · · · · · · · · · · · · · · · · · · 11
Chapter 4   We Try to Control Our World · · · · · · · · · · · 15
Chapter 5   Altruism Is Extremely Rare · · · · · · · · · · · · 19
Chapter 6   We Don't Know What Will Happen Next · · · 23
Chapter 7   G-d Runs the World · · · · · · · · · · · · · · · · 27
Chapter 8   Key to the Covenant · · · · · · · · · · · · · · · · 31
Chapter 9   Practice · 39
Chapter 10 Troubleshooting · · · · · · · · · · · · · · · · · · 59
Chapter 11 More Practice · 67

Conclusion · 87
About the Author · · · · · · · · · · · · · · · · · · · 89

INTRODUCTION

I REMEMBER THAT when I was about nine years old, I was fascinated by what makes people behave as they do. In high school more than one classmate asked me if I was going to be a psychiatrist. I went to medical school specifically to become one. I completed my formal training in psychiatry about twenty-five years ago; I have been in private practice since and have learned a lot. I've treated, counseled, and educated individuals, couples, and families as well as received feedback from them and my colleagues. The idea for this project has come from a common question I have been asked: "Where can I find this in a book?" With deference to Dr. McCoy, I commonly answer, "I'm a psychiatrist, not a librarian." My goal is for this text to be that book.

My path of becoming more observant in Judaism is described in my book *Arc of the Covenant*. This spiritual path is difficult to separate from my personal and professional development in psychiatry. Taken together, I have formulated some premises and conclusions for how to improve relationships. Relationships in this sense can be marriages, friendships, or other connections with other human beings.

On the pages that follow, I endeavor to put my thoughts into words so that if you can read it and practice the concepts laid out, then your relationships will improve significantly.

The chapter titles are things that I discovered in the course of my professional and personal life that strike me as incontrovertible and lend themselves to making my points. You may not buy all of the premises, but if you can tolerate them and hold on to the concepts that I try to convey, I will tie them all together at the end, and it will be palatable for even the most discerning tastes.

Finally, before we begin in earnest, let me make a comment about the title. There are many different ways to define what a covenant is. For now, let's consider it to be a special type of contract. In your average, run-of-the-mill contract, if one of the parties involved does not hold up his or her end, the contract is broken. Of course, contracts can have stipulations that describe what happens if one of the parties does not follow through with his or her responsibilities. I guess you could say the contract would still be enforceable and in place. I want to make a distinction that when I use the word "covenant," the relationship continues on, and on, and on. An example of what I have in mind would be the covenant between G-d and the Jewish people. L-rd knows we have messed up innumerable times, but we still have a covenant with G-d.

This concept of a covenant is commonly extended to include marriage. When somebody screws up, no matter how badly, you're still married. Obviously, there are things that can be done to dissolve that covenant, but for the sake of discussion, it takes some doing. It is probably fair to say that a covenant has more permanence to it than a contract when talking about relationships. The commitment inherent in a covenant is something that can be harnessed in other relationships to strengthen the bonds that then allow for healthier foundations or complete repair of damage.

CHAPTER 1

ALL COUPLES ARE EQUAL

A PHENOMENON THAT I noticed years ago was how equally matched every couple was that came to my office. This fact has proven to be very helpful for me as the clinician, and when my patients understand it, it's invariably helpful for them as well, but the concept can be a very difficult sell. Virtually all of the pairs that walk into the room think that their partner is the main problem. If that were not the case, and someone thought that he or she were him- or herself the issue, that person would have come for individual therapy.

Anyway, one of them will tell me what the problem is with the other person, and then I hear it from the other person, and its game on. I use my judgment as to when I explain the concept. It usually happens early in treatment, and it sounds something like this: "Every couple I have ever seen is equal. You show me someone who has a problem with an addiction, and I will show you the spouse who struggles with codependency. If you tell me about someone who has a problem with his temper, I will tell you that his partner has an equally difficult time expressing herself appropriately."

If I don't see eyes glazed over at this point, I continue. "If a couple walked in, and one of them was an attractive, intelligent, well-spoken individual, and the spouse was dumpy looking, unkempt, and not sounding so bright, I guarantee you that the good-looking one would be really messed up inside and that the one who looked messed up would have the soul of a tzaddik."

I have 50 percent affirmative head nods at this point but a 99.9 percent chance the concept will not be helpful to them yet. I persevere.

Because I remain convinced of the empirical validity of my observations, I will continue to point out the concept over time. What happens as I wear down one member or both members of the couple is that they begin to realize not only their own role in the dysfunction of the relationship but also that it is infinitely more efficient for them to work on their own junk instead of focusing on their partner's stuff.

How in the world does it happen that we match up with our equals? There are unconscious factors—forces that we are not aware of that bring us together. There exists some psychobabble about object-relations theory, transference reactions and some other stuff I could share, but let's just say for now there are forces that we are not consciously aware of when it comes to choosing a mate.

Marriage itself, using the old-fashioned definition, is an example. Today, marriage has become synonymous with union between two people. For the longest time, marriage was more specifically defined as a divinely inspired union between a man and a woman. Inherent in this latter definition is the concept that godly forces are at work bringing two people together. This perspective would certainly help explain further my idea that both people in a couple are equal.

Another way to understand the unconscious forces at work would be to consider that in a marriage, each member of the union can point to traits in the other that he or she has assumed. We are supposed to begin to look like each other after a while, right? Not just appearance, of course, but sayings, ideas, and attitudes. Likewise, couples who are together for a period of time will assume patterns of behavior that balance out the behaviors of their spouses. A simple example is the one above about the alcoholic and codependent. Another example would be when one spouse struggles with anger and the other backs out or withdraws with equal intensity or may dish it back like a volley in a tennis match.

This is hard to quantify, but it is as if there is a physical law of the universe that makes us respond to another equally. If you were sitting in front of me in my office, and I asked you to raise your hand up in front of you, and then I leaned forward and placed my hand against yours and began to gently push, there is a 100 percent guarantee that you would provide resistance to my pushing even though I didn't say or ask you to push.

I will tell you one way that I utilize this concept personally. It has happened maybe once or twice that my wife has done something, or not, that leaves me believing I am doing more than my fair share. I can remind myself that she carried both of our children to term and certainly did most of the childcare work when they were very young. I never had to be pregnant, give birth, or devote the quantity of time to the girls that she did early in their lives. During that time, I would have been sitting on a stool in the delivery room, playing basketball, or sleeping. It would take several lifetimes of hauling the trash to the front of the driveway to even the score.

When you can realize that there is equilibrium in the relationship, you are better able to deal with the feeling that all the weight is on you. The fact is that marriage is a team sport, and it requires a different perspective than if you were playing only as an individual. It is extremely unusual that the championship basketball team has the player who led the league in scoring on its roster.

At the same time, a balance is required so that you do not lose yourself or who you are. It helps, and is often necessary, to have someone outside of you to give you feedback on how you sound, look, or act. In my office for the past twenty years, I have hosted an informal weekly consultation group for myself and local therapists so that we can run situations by each other and expose ourselves to critiques from other clinicians. Whether it is a professional therapeutic relationship or one like a marriage, it is easy to lose track of your contributions to the success or dysfunction of the relationship. Having a source outside of you would invariably help keep your keel in the water and decrease the waves that you will create in the relationship. Remembering just how equal you are lends itself to more optimism that a balance can be found or restored.

This balance requires some boundaries to exist between you and the other person. The main tool to use so that this can happen is, in fact, the key to the covenant.

CHAPTER 2

EVERYTHING HAS A PROCESS AND A CONTENT

ONE OF THE things necessary to establish good boundaries and healthy communication in a relationship is to be able to speak and understand a common language. We all know what language we speak, and it really should not be very difficult to sort out whether the language coming back at you is the same as yours. What seems to be poorly understood by most of the inhabitants of this planet is that when we speak to each other, there is invariably both a process (the way we speak) and a content (the actual words we are using).

If I were to say to you, "You look nice," the content would be those three words. If I were to roll my eyes when I said those three words, then the meaning would be very different than if I were to look at you with a sincere face. The process is the way I say those three words—my manner, or my behavior, or the tone of voice that I am using.

It is a toss-up as to which is more important. We have heard that a picture is worth a thousand words. This saying would seem to support the idea that process is more important. Yet at the same time, we know how powerful—whether they are healing or hurtful—just a few words can be. Having good boundaries in a relationship will help immeasurably in understanding both process and content and vice versa.

Follow along with me here. If a wife asks her husband to change the light bulb in the kitchen, and he forgets to do it, she asks again. So he doesn't do it this time and goes off to work. He comes home. The wife is upset because the kitchen is still dark. How many different problems do we have here? If you answered two, then you understand process and content.

If you answered something else or just kept reading without pausing, contemplating, and answering as you were told to do, you should continue to read this chapter.

So there are two problems. One, the wife is upset. Two, the light bulb needs to be changed. If the husband were to come home and be greeted by an angry wife, and then he were to say OK and change the light bulb, I would bet a nickel that she would still be angry. On the other hand, if he responds to the process and acknowledges what is going on and how upset she is, that may assuage her anger, but then they are still both standing in a dark room.

Dealing with a situation like this could prompt someone to use the F-word—"feelings." Maybe even the other F-word—"frustration." In general, guys are more content oriented, while women are more process oriented. Wanting to fix something or change a light bulb is more about the content. What it feels like is about the process. The trouble with feelings is that they don't usually lend themselves to being fixed, especially in another person.

Feelings can be frustrating for the person experiencing them, but the frustration would be even greater if one were to try to fix someone else's feelings. I contend that it's impossible to be responsible for someone else's feelings—like it is impossible to be responsible for the climate. We can certainly pollute less, but manage or control the weather—I think not. Another way to say this is that I am responsible for my behavior but not your feelings. You are welcome to opine that my behavior might have made you feel whatever you feel, but it's not reasonable to ascribe responsibility to me for those feelings.

For example, if I were to purposely step on your foot out of the blue, I would anticipate that you might be upset, shocked, surprised, or angry. I would contend that I am not responsible for those feelings. I am responsible for my boorish behavior, for which there may well be a consequence headed my way. Indirect proof of this would be that if I were to apologize, kiss your toes, or make amends in some other fashion, which I might do if the feelings were my responsibility, you may still remain upset, shocked, surprised, or angry. Also, for all we know you might have been someone a little odd who took pleasure in my sadistic act.

It comes up all the time in relationships where one person says to the other, "You should have known that would make me feel..." You can add whatever feeling you'd like in there. Not true. And this will come up again in another context in the next chapter.

You might ask, "So what was that guy with the light bulb supposed to do?" He was supposed to know both languages. To practice speaking or listening to any language will improve vocabulary and understanding. Achieving a balance between communicating in process or content is going to come more naturally to you when you understand the key to the covenant.

CHAPTER 3

EVERYTHING ANYBODY EVER DOES MAKES SENSE TO THEM

I EXPECT THAT most of us experience this on a daily basis: Somebody does something that doesn't make sense to us. We ask ourselves or incredulously say out loud, "Why did he [or you] do that?" People do things all the time that seem to defy explanation. In every one of those situations, without exception, the behavior made sense to the person doing it.

Think about what you have done today. Not everything may have worked out the way you wanted it to, but everything you did make sense at the time you did it...otherwise, you would not have done it. For better or worse, we tend to be very accepting of our own behavior. We may regret our behavior or feel guilty about it, but that is invariably after the fact. Consider even a situation where you tell yourself, "I shouldn't do this." When you do it anyway, I trust that you can appreciate that obviously there were conscious or unconscious forces that prompted you to act accordingly.

Keeping this in mind will allow for more patience and tolerance in any relationship. It is also a concept that will make it easier to take things less personally. When you think that someone did not take your feelings into account, consider that his or her actions were about him- or herself and not you. Again, trust me on this, it is not intuitively obvious, but it made sense to them to do exactly what they did. The guy who did not change the light bulb certainly had something else on his mind. We can hypothesize that he had something else he would rather have done, or maybe he intended to change the light bulb and just forgot and did something else instead. In both cases, what he did made sense to him, and it was not about his wife. Let's consider a very sinister angle: that he purposefully and therefore maliciously did not change the light bulb because he wanted to have a negative effect on his wife. Here again, this example would fit with the premise of this chapter. For whatever reason we can imagine, it made sense to *him* to not change the bulb.

By better understanding this principle, you will have better interpersonal boundaries that I said before were so important. Consider how helpful it would be if we would not take as many things personally as we do. By definition, taking something personally means that we think it is about us. Invariably this would be somebody else's speech or behavior. Notice what would happen if we conceptualize the other's behavior as a function of that person and not us. If it made sense to that individual, that means it sure as heck was not about me.

You may ask, "How could it not be about me if they are looking right at me and talking right at me?" And I would answer, "How could it possibly be about you if it's coming out of them?" If you can see it or hear it, then it is not yours; it belongs to someone else. You are responsible for your thoughts, speech, and actions. Straightforward, right? Well, that should also be true about the other person as well. Another way to look at this would be to consider someone giving you his or her political opinion. That's not *about you*, is it? What would be the difference between somebody's political opinion and his or her opinion about you? There is no difference; both are the opinions of the person who is talking—and neither is about you.

If this concept still doesn't make sense, I encourage you to reread this section and consider it further. It is not a make-it-or-break-it concept, but being able to keep this in mind will definitely make it easier to make use of the key to the covenant.

CHAPTER 4

WE TRY TO CONTROL OUR WORLD

CONSISTENT WITH WHAT I described in the last chapter, we tend to personalize things. That is really not much of a surprise considering that most of us were treated as if we were the center of the universe the first couple years of our lives, and it's not always so easy to unlearn this. Everybody is looking at us, wants to hold us, tend to our every need, and drop what they're doing when we come in the room. After that, it goes downhill in the I-am-the-center-of-the-world department. People start telling us no, and they seem to have other things to do besides pay attention to us. It's just not as good as it used to be. By the way, this is what the terrible twos are all about. It's certainly not about being two; it's about heretofore those kids got everything they wanted, and now they don't, and that doesn't go over well. So they cry, fuss, and throw a fit. Some of this results in them getting what they want, and you'll never guess what happens then: they repeat the ostentatious behavior since it worked for them before.

This is a good spot to understand where procrastination comes from. Some of us stumble onto the concept that if we dawdle a little bit, we actually regain some of the control we have lost. Mom tells the kid, "C'mon, it's time to go." Kid then dillydallies and Mom gets upset. Kid discovers that horsing around—that is, procrastinating—puts him back in control. Then even if the kid is punished for not getting ready right away, his two- or three-year-old brain might prefer the sense of control over the potential punishment. Lots of us continue to do stuff like that into adulthood but lose track of why we started to procrastinate in the first place. We were trying to regain control of our lives and to manage the people around us.

Further solidifying toddlerhood as a time for dysfunctional adaptation, this is the time when we are toilet trained. We are being asked to perform bodily functions at the whim and will of our parents, something that should be 100 percent our deal. We think to ourselves, *Mom and Dad are telling me to pee and poop. I'll be the judge of that!* And so the battle lines get drawn. Some of us escape this battle zone relatively unscathed with some developmental adaptations that serve us well. Others crash and burn for a while. Final results of personality formation TBD.

I hope you will be able to see that calling someone a control freak doesn't really set him or her apart from anybody else since we all try to control our worlds. If you are intellectually honest with yourself, you will be able to understand your own personality and recognize that so much of your own behavior can be understood in terms of controlling or regulating distance between yourself and others, trying to get your way, and not being subjugated to the will of someone else.

There are lots of shapes and sizes here. It is easy to understand how this applies to someone who is angry or aggressive. I anticipate you know somebody who you think is "controlling" but might be very passive instead. How about somebody who is pleasant and easy to get along with? Recognize that the positive traits probably work very well for them when it comes to controlling their environment. They are blessed (and so are we to know them) that they have discovered how to manage things in their world and be very pleasant and likable at the same time.

Maybe you are thinking that you know plenty of people, maybe even yourself, who are not so controlling. In fact, you would argue that there are all kinds of good-natured people who give of themselves or donate their time, energy, and money without expecting anything in return. How in the world can that be controlling? There are two parts to this answer: First, I don't think they really did not expect anything in return, which I will write more about in the next chapter. Second, even if you don't accept what I'm going to explain next, keeping this matter in mind will better help you utilize the key to the covenant.

CHAPTER 5

ALTRUISM IS EXTREMELY RARE

IN FACT, I am not sure if altruism exists anywhere on the planet. I don't want you to misunderstand me; there are oodles of good people who do good things all the time. I just think that it is next to impossible to do something that is not motivated by something self-serving. For those of you who agree with this position, you are welcome to skip to the next chapter. Everybody else, let me belabor the point.

When you gave to charity, did you expect something in return? Sure about that? Did you get a receipt for tax purposes? OK, fine, you are not taking a tax deduction. Did you expect a thank-you? All right, you did not expect anything. You took a cash donation and put it in a plain, unmarked envelope and left it outside your rabbi's house, knocked on the door, and ran away before you could be seen or identified. So, my egalitarian friend, you made this donation with no expectation of anything in return? No, I don't think so. Even in this extreme case, I anticipate that you made this anonymous donation because it was going to benefit you in some way. Maybe this would be a way to have G-d's countenance shine down upon you. Maybe it is just as simple as you would feel better. Whatever the case, there was something in it for you.

Why do I make such a big deal about this? I'll tell you. When it comes to working with couples or improving relationships, it helps tremendously when we can sort out what is my stuff and what is yours. When somebody says, "I did that for you," or "I was thinking of you," it adds to the confusion if we have to separate self-proclaimed righteousness, kindness, selflessness, and selfishness. Appreciating that there is no altruism makes it easier to understand and integrate some of the concepts previously described, like how we try to control our world and that everything makes sense to the person who actually did the act. Not subscribing to the concept of altruism in relationships encourages individuals to be more reflective of their own behavior and motivation behind it. Taking responsibility for your own thoughts, feelings, and actions is a cornerstone to healthy relationships.

Well, that is all fine and good that I am responsible for my own stuff, but what about him or her? Aye, there's the rub. In order for there to be a relationship, there's got to be two involved. What can we do if the other person is not holding up his or her end of the bargain? That is a great question! And it has an answer. And that answer will be developed more over the next two chapters, which, taken together, will fill in the final pieces necessary to recognize, understand, and benefit from the key to the covenant.

CHAPTER 6

WE DON'T KNOW WHAT WILL HAPPEN NEXT

YOU PROBABLY CAN readily agree with this statement. And likely would not argue with me about its merits. However, I don't recall meeting anybody who actually believes this when the rubber hits the road. We all anticipate what is going to happen—it's natural and a good survival instinct. But more times than not, we get into trouble when we lose track of the fact that we do this in our relationships. Who hasn't thought they know how someone is going to react if such and such happens or such and such is said? In fact, it's quite common that patients will assert with absolute certainty that they know what their spouse, son, daughter, or parents will do in a given situation. I am positive that they don't know. In fact, I have never lost a bet with my patients who insist they know what's going to happen.

Before they find themselves in a virtual no-win situation, I have often suggested that they try the following test: Take a small three-by-five-inch spiral notebook and start writing down your predictions of what someone is going to say or do. Feel free to make predictions in situations in which you are remarkably sure. What you will find is that you are horrible at predicting people's behavior, even for those people who are extremely close to you. If you don't heed my advice and do this little experiment, you may be in a situation where you tell me that you know what your spouse (for example) will say if you say such and such. I bet you five dollars that this will not be the case. After the conversation takes place, I end up with five dollars. I have found my patients initially to be extremely confident when it comes to knowing what somebody else is going to do. Turns out they don't. Unfortunately, we all tend to remember the times when we were right in these situations much more than when we were wrong.

This phenomenon is a major impediment to having a healthy relationship. Plus, nobody appreciates it when you tell him or her that you know what he or she is going to do or say in a given situation. Even in retrospect, when you say to somebody, "I knew you would do that," it is not usually part of a friendly interaction.

Understanding this particular concept will help you in a variety of ways. Once you realize that you don't know what's going to happen, decision making becomes easier. A major reason we get stuck and can't decide on something is that we were worried about a bad outcome. Well, what makes you think you know what's going to happen? There is certainly room for good judgment and discretion to influence your decision making, but thinking you know the outcome ahead of time should not be a feature of that process. Another feature of this perspective is that you will now become freer to express your own opinions or feelings. Who better to represent these two items than you? Trying to manage the opinions and feelings of another person based on what you *think* the person will say or do takes away from your opportunity to represent something you should know much more about: you! This distinction will also facilitate some psychological space that will be needed if the other person is not as invested as he or she could be in the relationship. By having more clarity regarding what is yours versus theirs, you will be in a far better position to represent your own thoughts and ideas while simultaneously respecting theirs.

How do we get the other person to respect our thoughts and feelings? There is no better rule than the golden rule. Do unto others as you would want them to do unto you. You want respect? Give it. Want investment in a relationship from someone else? Do it. Not satisfied with that? It will serve you well to have constant awareness of what ultimately makes our relationships, which will be the final piece to understanding the key to the covenant.

CHAPTER 7

G-D RUNS THE WORLD

THERE IS A lot of circumstantial evidence to support this; suffice it to say that if you don't already agree with this supposition, it is important to work on adopting a similar understanding. *The Big Book of Alcoholics Anonymous* has a chapter for agnostics. The concept there is described as accepting there is a force in the universe greater than you. Being able to do that will help you understand what's necessary to accomplish in this chapter.

For those of you who don't think or know that G-d runs the world, I hope that the AA concept is easier to accept. It should be intuitively obvious that the weather, direction of the stock market, alignment of the planets, and so on are not things you can manage. If you think that burning wood, buying a whole bunch of Google stock, or jumping up and down really high can affect those things in any measurable fashion, I want to tell you that you have serious skills. I'm hoping that you can appreciate that there is a lot that you don't control. If you're with me on this so far, I'd like to jump ahead to the bottom line: you don't control diddly squat.

Sure, we have free will and the ability to constantly make choices and effect our environment, but it's invariably the case that the outcome of any event that we are involved with depends on more than just our choice or will. For those of you who believe that G-d runs the world but we don't have free will or choice, I will remind you that G-d is infinite not only in space but in time as well. That means G-d exists in the future at the same time as the present moment; so G-d knows what will happen. His existence in future time, as well as the accompanying knowledge of events that will take place, does not take away the fact that we get to do pretty much whatever we darn well please. We just have no control whatsoever outside of our own thoughts, feelings, and actions.

Of course, there are exceptions there too. For example, please, *don't* think of an elephant. You know the big, gray mammal with big ears and a trunk. You probably did just picture an elephant. We have some control but not complete mastery over all our thoughts, feelings, and actions. I am sure we can remember instances when we were overcome by feelings we could not seem to manage, and we certainly have involuntary tics or movements. But we do get to make choices all the time; we just don't get to control the outcome.

This is so important to understand in relationships but so difficult to actually get clear in our brains. We have touched on this before in the chapter about how you don't know what the other person is going to do. That's another way of saying there are forces outside of our control that affect our world. That is another way of saying that G-d runs the world. Here again, it is not necessary that you subscribe to the idea that the Almighty has a role in what happens on a day-to-day basis. For those of you who do, an extra bonus feature of that belief is the satisfaction that the world is created in such a way that it is biased in the direction for us to do the right thing. The greatest gift we have from our Creator might be the multiple ways we have been given to fix our screw-ups. Understanding that G-d knows what will happen—and He has the power to destroy like He does to create—obviously we have been granted multiple mulligans and do overs. We can say further that since He knows what we will do and what we think, He then certainly gets us and understands us. You are also welcome to take significant consolation in the fact that things will work out the way they are supposed to, the way G-d understands already that they are going to play out.

The golden rule alluded to in the last chapter is based on the biblical verse in Leviticus that translates as, "You should love your fellow as yourself. I am G-d." It is easy to see how that first sentence relates to the rule. The second sentence takes it to another level. It is not just what we say and do, but how we think and feel, which are understood by G-d. His omnipotence insures that our efforts to comply with the rule result in direct benefit.

For those of you I started to lose when I was talking about G-d, please integrate this: there is a limit to what you can control and manage. If you wanted to improve your relationships, there are things that you can do, but you can't do it all by yourself; you need some other things that fall into place, and they are not under your control. I'm going to ask you to respect that force that is above and beyond you, whether you give it a name or not.

It would be lovely if we were all together at this point because I want to tie things up and explain the main reason we have gathered here today. Holding in mind the above discussion, as well as the concepts previously laid out, makes it far more likely that you will be able to integrate what is about to follow.

CHAPTER 8

KEY TO THE COVENANT

THE KEY TO the covenant is empathy. That is simple enough. The trouble is very few people get this. If everybody did, we would bring on the messianic age pretty darn quick. I believe I have laid the groundwork for you to get this concept, and I want to put it together for you in a package to enable you to significantly improve all your relationships and help all of mankind out as well.

Let's start with a clear definition. Empathy is the active process of conveying to another person that you get what it's like to be him or her. Empathy is not feeling what someone else feels. That's impossible. There is no way that you could ever know if you felt what someone else felt. There might be a flash or even longer when you did feel what someone else felt, but how in the world could you possibly know that? Empathy is also not sympathy. Sympathy is about your own feelings. *You* feel sorry. Empathy is about the *other* person's feelings and, just as importantly, that you can demonstrate that you understand that person.

Let's break the definition down. The first part is the active process. This differs from being passive. Active implies that you are going to use intonation of your voice, body language, or facial expression to convey your message. What is your message? That you know what it is like to be them. How would you know that? Well, you could ask, or listen, or look. You would use your brain to come up with a reasonable idea of what it's like to be the other person, and then you would actively communicate that. This definition allows you to empathize with someone even though you might not have had the same experience. If a Vietnam veteran was telling me a story or experience from the war, I certainly don't know what he feels like while telling me the story, and I certainly don't know what it was like to be there. However, I can integrate how he looks and what I hear and then convey that back to him. I remember a former marine telling me how he would use a lit cigar to burn off some of the leeches that had attached to him during the night. Most all of us will have some independent reaction to hearing this, but to be empathic, it is important to try to get a sense of what that was like for him, not just being there but also in telling the story. When you then use your own words to express or mirror that back to him, you are empathizing.

This is not to be confused with active listening, which merely requires good eye contact and head nods and maybe a well-timed "uh-huh." Empathy is more dynamic and interactive. It's important when you empathize that you continue to listen. If the person you are empathizing with nods his or her head in agreement, seems to relax, or acknowledges appreciation, you've likely empathized well. But if the person you're trying to be empathic with says, "No, that's not it" or looks at you like you are from outer space, you may want to try again or simply ask the person to help you understand what it's like to be him or her. Notice again, please, that empathy is about the other person—it's not about you.

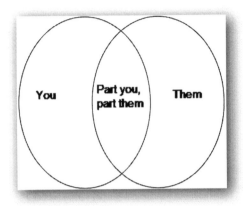

What happens in relationships as they deepen and become more significant is that boundaries become more blurred. Looking at the Venn diagram here, you can see that the amount of overlap is indicative of the lack of boundaries in the relationship. Also understand that the amount of overlap in this pictorial will be dependent on a multitude of factors, including the people involved, the situation at hand, and the length of time that the relationship has existed. It's usually the case that the more overlap there is, the deeper the relationship. The deeper relationship will be associated with more relationship angst. In marriage, there is a lot of overlap. In this type of relationship, you can lose yourself, which is not usually a good thing. Fixing the relationship, or at least improving it, is usually dependent on boundaries being improved. Empathy is the best single tool to use to improve boundaries in a relationship. Anything that will help you and the other person understand what is yours and what is theirs will facilitate this effort. You have to sell it, believe it, live it, and breathe it. The more you think about empathy as being about the other person—which means it's going to take some work on your part to get it and then convey it—the more valuable it will be for you and the other person. Empathy can therefore be self-serving, and that's OK.

Another great thing about empathy is that it does so many other things besides facilitate boundaries. Empathy also helps to soothe the other person. This is a really good idea since the diagrams represent that the other person is a part of you, and marriage is a team sport. You benefit when your teammate does well.

In any relationship, there is an equilibrium that is created. It may not always be comfortable or even healthy. Again, being empathic can restore health to an enmeshed relationship by improving boundaries. It can also blur boundaries in a good way by conveying unconditional love. If you think about what unconditional love is, you will likely end up with a definition close to how I define empathy since by my definition, empathy is selfless and directed at understanding and accepting the other person as he or she is.

As a reminder, empathy is not admitting that the other person is right. Recall our political example from earlier. Conveying that you understand someone else's opinion in an empathic way acknowledges that you understand his or her opinion, and that opinion could well be different than yours.

Even though I have hammered away at empathy being about the other person, you will also help yourself in a variety of ways by being empathic. Being empathic toward another person is a great way to deal with your own defensiveness. If someone accuses you of something, the normal response is going to be to deny or maybe to question the other person about his or her accusation. Both of those responses would be making the issue more about you. We run the risk of being defensive in such a situation, which is cured by being empathic. This is because when you are empathic, neither the content nor the process of the conversation is about you. You are now speaking about and, if done effectively, having feelings that direct your attention away from your own experience to that of the other person. Similarly, if your feelings are hurt, which would be about you, keep in mind that everything anybody ever says or does makes sense to that person. The intention was not to hurt you; it's much more likely that his or her behavior was about his or her anger, frustration, or whatever. The more you get that, the less your feelings will be hurt.

Also consider the possibility that you might be angry. Most of the time when we are angry, it's concerning someone else. In order to be angry with someone else, you've got to be connected. Figuratively disconnecting by being empathic will invariably result in you having less angry feelings.

Empathy is also the foundation of what's necessary to effect change in another person. Can you remember listening to any type of call-in radio show where psychological advice is doled out? It's common that the caller will offer some explanation or excuse why the advice he or she is given will not work. Let's call that resistance to change. This resistance will be lowered if that person has a sense that the advice giver truly understands what he or she is going through. It's easy to see this in my practice. If a patient came in and told me what was wrong, and I told him or her how to fix it, that would probably help about one out of every hundred people. What is far more effective is when I convey to them first some empathic understanding of their problem. The empathy itself is often enough to have curative value since often people know what would be best for them or can figure out a problem themselves with emotional support. The empathy serves as the support to that process. If my counsel or advice is counterintuitive to them, there is no way it will help unless the patients believe that I get them and what they are going through, what has been their experiences, or the difficulties they've had in solving the problem so far.

It is not reasonable to expect you or anybody else to always be empathic. That type of altruism can only be theoretical for humans, though we can strive for something more. There is some biblical exegesis that is worth referencing to make this point. G-d has a covenantal relationship with the Jewish people. The circumstantial evidence on the table is that this relationship still exists because we continue to be here despite innumerable attempts to get rid of us over time. Two of the names used for G-d in the Hebrew Bible are Elokim and YHVH. The former is understood to be associated with nature and other finite concepts. The latter is understood to be synonymous with the infinite. It is significant that the latter name for G-d is used in the Bible when talking about compassion and mercy. The former is associated with our creation. Our finite nature is physical and emotional. However, this does not have to be the case with our kindness and benevolence. Working to perfect our world by infusing godliness or the infinite is a holy and noble endeavor, to say the least.

Empathy is key in a covenantal relationship. To achieve such a permanent connection, there needs to be a way to work out problems, to unconditionally accept the other person, and to be able to effectively deal with anger, frustration, and hurt feelings—in other words, to convey those infinite qualities. Understanding and practicing empathy in our relationships is the key to that pursuit.

CHAPTER 9

PRACTICE

IF SOMEBODY SHOWED you exactly how to do a perfect golf swing, there is no way you're going to be ready for the PGA Tour unless you practice a ton. Same thing here. To facilitate empathy training, I've written some vignettes with a solution on the page that follows. Think about the situation for a moment before you read my answer. There will be other ways to solve the problems, but I hope that my suggestions will serve to make you think about the process I have outlined in the preceding chapters and better enable you to put the concepts into play yourself.

1. YOU ARE HAVING AN ARGUMENT OR DISCUSSION BACK AND FORTH, CLEARLY
    STATING YOUR POINT OF VIEW, BUT THE OTHER PERSON, (THIS CAN BE A
    SPOUSE, PARTNER, FRIEND, OR SOMEONE YOU MET FIVE MINUTES AGO), JUST
    DOESN'T SEEM TO GET IT. WHAT CAN YOU DO DIFFERENTLY?

Do unto others as you would want them to do unto you. Go out of your way to demonstrate that you understand *the other person's* point of view. Under no circumstance—and this is an absolute—say the word "but" when you go about conveying this. It's very easy to fall into this trap when you empathize with another person you disagree with. Since it is important to you that he or she understands what you're saying, you will contrast your empathic understanding of his or her position with the word "but" in order to express again what your thoughts or feelings are. This would put you right back where you started, with the other person invariably having the impression that you don't in fact understand his or her position.

Keep in mind that the argument he or she is making undoubtedly makes sense to that person even though it makes no sense to you. Try your best to generate respect for that other person and the fact that, however he or she went about it, he or she came to this particular conclusion. It's your task now to convey that you appreciate his or her position. Remember, you don't have to agree with that position, but you do have to be able to demonstrate that you understand where the person is coming from.

2. YOU ARE AT A FUNERAL FOR SOMEONE WHO HAS DIED TRAGICALLY. YOU ARE
    AT A LOSS FOR WHAT YOU CAN SAY TO THE FAMILY MEMBERS. WHAT CAN
    YOU SAY OR DO?

It would be great to convey unconditional love to the family and friends of the deceased. Empathy is clearly the best way to do that. Trying to understand what it's like for someone who has lost a loved one tragically is very difficult to grasp or understand, especially if you have not been through this yourself. An important point to make here is that empathy can be conveyed by action alone. Don't lose track of the importance of just being there. You don't have to say anything. It may be helpful for you to remember that there is so much we don't control in our world around us. Don't try to fix anything here; just try your best to understand what those who are grieving are going through, and just try to be there.

KEY TO THE COVENANT

3.   YOU JUST SAT DOWN ON THE COUCH AND TURNED ON THE GAME. YOUR SPOUSE
     COMES IN THE FRONT DOOR AND YELLS AT YOU TO COME AND HELP WITH THE
     GROCERIES. WHAT CAN YOU SAY OR DO?

Get off your butt and go help. Sure, you can yell back that you just sat down. Recognize that if you do, you are helping set up a classic process-versus-content scenario. The content is that groceries need to get from the car to kitchen. At this point how this is going to happen is not clear. That is part of the process. The other part of the process are the potential feelings which are percolating for you, the couch sitter, and the spouse who asks for help and does not receive it. If this situation escalates or blows up on you, you will want to try to keep the process/content dichotomy in mind as you try to dig yourself out.

4. YOUR FIVE-YEAR-OLD WANTS A BALLOON IN THE STORE. YOU SAY NO. THE KID
    STARTS TO CRY AND MAKE A SCENE. WHAT DO YOU DO?

Sure, you can say no. Sure, you can leave the store. Want to spank him? Whatever. However, you can also convey that you get him. He wants the balloon and likes the balloon. Let him know that you get that. The tricky part is not saying "but" here. That would be like erasing the empathic understanding you just conveyed. The challenge is to make your thought or feeling separate in the conversation. There will be plenty of other times to educate him regarding proper in-store behavior. "You want that balloon?" [Point to it.] "No wonder you do; it's a really neat one." [Pause. Sad, sorry face.] "I've got bad news. We came to the store for milk. This won't be a trip to get a balloon." Chances are that the situation is more tolerable now.

5. THERE IS SOMEONE AT WORK WHO IS MEAN SPIRITED. SHE JUST SAID
    SOMETHING VERY CRITICAL THAT INSINUATED YOU DID SOMETHING WRONG.
    BESIDES ARGUING OR DEFENDING YOURSELF, WHAT CAN YOU DO?

You can realize that what she just said is all about her. It is not about you. It was *her* opinion that she just shared, as well as *her* behavior that was mean spirited. Five will get you ten that she is upset, angry, or irritated. Demonstrate that you understand this (without saying the word "but"). Besides that, it made sense to her to say or do as she did. That's her deal. The more you get this concept, the less you will be affected by her words and actions. Remember also that actually saying it in a sincere fashion like "It seems to me that this really bothers you a lot" is much better than just thinking or being aware of it.

6.   YOU RUN A BUSY ANIMAL RESCUE. YOU GET A CALL FROM SOMEONE WHO IS
     MOVING IN JUST A COUPLE OF DAYS, AND HE WANTS YOU TO TAKE HIS PET
     AND FIND IT A HOME. YOU ARE FRUSTRATED BY THE FACT THAT HE WAITED
     UNTIL THE LAST MINUTE, AND TAKING THIS PET ON WILL SEVERELY TAX YOUR
     RESOURCES. WHAT CAN YOU DO?

It will help you first to realize that your frustration comes from what *he* did and that it made sense *to him* to wait until now to call you. His choices and behavior is about him and not you. He is trying to manage and control his world. Your job is to run your shelter and manage your own feelings. *You* are welcome to take into account your resources, the needs of the pet, the owners, and so on and make your best determination of what to do with Fido. He has to deal with whatever your actions will be.

7. YOU HAVE MADE A BIG CHANGE IN YOUR LIFE, LIKE A DECISION TO CHANGE JOBS OR LOSE SIGNIFICANT WEIGHT. YOU GET COMMENTS FROM PEOPLE CLOSE TO YOU THAT YOU DID THE WRONG THING BY CHANGING JOBS OR THAT YOU HAVE LOST TOO MUCH WEIGHT. HOW CAN YOU HANDLE THIS?

You should be able to nail this, now. It's about them. It's their opinions and not only that—it's their decisions to share their opinions with you. Their decisions to share can be from a place of concern or jealousy. For your purposes, it doesn't matter. Let's let it be about them. Tell them, "You sound concerned." If it fits better, say, "You sound upset about my decision." Either way, the strategy is to help you not take their comments personally.

8. YOU HAVE A FRIEND WHO IS NOT CALLING BACK, AND YOU WOULD LIKE THE RELATIONSHIP TO WORK OUT BUT ARE HAVING WORRIES AND NOW ALSO SOME DOUBTS THAT THE RELATIONSHIP IS WORTH SAVING. HOW CAN YOU BETTER DEAL WITH THE SITUATION?

You can try to get her behavior from her perspective. Essentially, understand the foundation of what an empathic understanding would be. She is not talking to you, so you can't actually empathize. However, you can realize that whether she calls back is not something you can control or manage. You get to decide if you want to wait or terminate. To facilitate the former, try to appreciate the infinite nature of compassion. This will likely help you tolerate the wait since being empathic can be in and of itself its own reward.

9. YOU WANT TO GO SKIING THREE HOURS AWAY. YOU TELL YOUR FRIENDS, AND
    THEY THINK IT'S A GREAT IDEA TOO. WITHOUT MAKING SURE THAT THE PLANS
    WORK WITH YOU, THEY BUY NONREFUNDABLE TICKETS AND GET A RENTAL
    CAR FOR ALL OF YOU. YOU CAN'T EVEN GO ON THAT DAY. NOW THEY ARE MAD
    AT YOU THAT THEY WASTED THEIR MONEY.

To help you utilize empathy, which allows you some psychological distance from their anger, it is helpful to keep in mind that there is no such thing as altruism. Conceding the reasonable possibility that your friends are caring and courteous, they still bought the tickets for their benefit. It fit their plans and schedule. The fact that they are upset that their plan did not work out the way they wanted it to is not your responsibility. For your benefit, you can say that you appreciate how frustrated they are since they thought it would work out well for everybody. It is a good thing for them, too, that you understand their feelings on the matter.

CHAPTER 10

TROUBLESHOOTING

LET'S STOP FOR a moment and go over some things. It won't surprise me if you have been able to breeze through the text and practice questions without too much stress or strain. It *would* surprise me if you have it all down now and were able to employ these skills without a hitch. My patients usually need more than one session to pull it all together. I want to review three issues that seem to come up regularly as impediments to putting this all together in real life.

The first is fear. Fear is the biggest reason why it is difficult to put these concepts into practice. It's always a good idea to refrain from saying something that you consider to be dumb, inappropriate, or unnecessary. On the other hand, not expressing yourself because you are afraid of the outcome is not a best-case scenario.

Being afraid or fearful leaves us feeling vulnerable, and that is no fun at all. However, we admire other people who are vulnerable. We are impressed by people who stand up for themselves, take risks, (to a point), or valiantly struggle with overwhelming feelings. It's easier to leave things the way they are and not take any chances, or maybe just complain. We are highly adaptable yet resistant to change.

If you think this applies to you, I encourage you to revisit the Table of Contents and pick out a chapter or two and reread them. Most everything I have talked about addresses this problem indirectly. Ultimately, to have these principles work for you, you will have to take a risk. So far, the act of reading this book has brought you face-to-face with very little risk. I tell my patients that the absolute biggest problem they will face if they take a chance and try to empathize with another person is that they can be accused of sounding like Dr. Fine. Take it from me, that's really not a very big deal.

The second issue that seems to come up often for people is the concern that empathizing does not allow for explaining one's own position. How will anybody understand what I want or need if I'm focused on them? That is certainly a fair question, and the answer is there needs to be some type of balance. If you have problems or difficulties in a relationship and all you did was empathize, that would be a bit weird. There has to be room for you to express your own thoughts or feelings.

How to actually do that is something you will discover yourself and it will be based on your own tolerance for risk, how you manage your fears, and the attitude and aptitude of the person to whom you are trying to relate. It may be helpful to keep in mind that when you express your own feelings, you will always be right. Keep in mind that your opinion, however, will always be arguable. Let's go over this in more detail. There are two tests you can employ to determine if something is a feeling or an opinion. The first is that feelings are one word long; happy, glad, scared, anxious, and frightened are all feelings. Opinions on the other hand are always more than one word long. The second test to distinguish between a feeling and an opinion is that feelings are never arguable and opinions are always arguable. So if I would say, "I feel that you don't like me," is that a feeling or an opinion?

It is an opinion. It is more than one word long, ("you don't like me"), and it is certainly arguable. You could say to me, "Sure I like you." What if I were to give an opinion that would be universally agreed upon like "Nuclear weapons are dangerous." Well, someone could argue that they are safe and a good idea to have around. But what if I were to tell you that I felt sad? It's silly to think that someone could argue that I'm not sad. I encourage people to recognize these difference and express feelings by saying, "I feel…" and to express opinions by saying, "I think…" Making this distinction will give you more confidence when you express yourself. You will be able to anticipate that if you share a feeling, it is rock solid and very easy to defend. If you were to express an opinion, please anticipate it is reasonable for the other person to disagree or have a very different perspective. With this distinction in mind, you are hereby empowered to better represent yourself.

Another impediment to expressing yourself and your position can be a self-inflicted wound caused by bringing up a third person. When we talk to another person about ourselves or them, the issue is right there in the room. If we bring somebody else into the discussion, whether we are referring to them or saying something that they said, things get complicated quickly. Not talking about a third person is very doable to put into practice, but if you haven't paid attention to it before you are likely to routinely be making this mistake. The next time you are in a difficult discussion, listen carefully to what you are saying. Did you bring a third person into it? If you did, get back to just the two of you. Of course, you can have a talk with somebody about a third person or something that they said. Just like you can have a corkscrew on your inflatable raft. You just have to know there is a risk involved and you should have a plan if you spring a leak.

The third issue with which people seem to routinely struggle is how to determine when to end a relationship. This book is about repairing relationships – very different than abandoning, trashing, nuking or terminating a relationship. To help with this problem, I have described for patients that if you have one black flag then you should end the relationship. A black flag is one of the three disaster signs: if there is ongoing physical or emotional abuse, an untreated substance abuse disorder, or ongoing infidelity. Or, if you have three red flags you should also end the relationship. What is a red flag? Showing up late all the time, not being trustworthy or reliable, anger problems, etc. Those are red flags, not black ones. We might also have a lesser violation, which we can call a pink flag. You have my blessings to tolerate as many pink flags as you can handle. Whatever the measure, it's going to be up to you to decide on the very personal question of when enough is enough.

I would admit the flag system is a simplistic way to evaluate a relationship, but it does lend some content to the process of struggling with the difficult decision of when to call it a day. This is another reason why conceptualizing relationships as a covenant can be helpful. Obviously if the relationship ends, there is not going to be much incentive or opportunity to work on it anymore. We want our relationships to last and prosper and that will include hanging in there despite some colored flags. That being said, I sincerely hope that if you went out with somebody on a first date and you noticed three red flags, there would not be a second date.

Here's another way to think about these issues: By being empathic you are protecting yourself by improving your interpersonal boundaries. Hence, from this position of strength, you will be in a better position to represent yourself with your feelings and/or your opinions. Trust me on this, when you understand the difference between your feelings (which you can express) and the other person's feelings (with which you can empathize) and you know the difference between process and content, you are like a Jedi Knight and can navigate any interpersonal situation that may arise. You are also acting as a role model. The best way to teach someone else about these skills would be to demonstrate them yourself. Whether or not the other person can learn from you or benefit from your improved communication skills could itself be a factor in the decision process as you try to sort out if the relationship is worth maintaining.

It's time to get back to the practice questions. Forgive me for stating the obvious: there are too many problems that come up in relationships to put down on paper in the form of question and answer. Working problems like this will be helpful, but pale in comparison to the value of trying this stuff out in real life. Keep going through what I've got here, try to imagine your own questions and answers, but most importantly get out there and mix it up yourself.

CHAPTER 11

MORE PRACTICE

10. YOU AND YOUR SIBLINGS ARE HAVING PROBLEMS AMONGST YOURSELVES DEALING WITH YOUR PARENTS. IT HAS TO DO WITH WHAT YOU THINK YOUR PARENTS SAID AND WHAT THEY WANT FROM YOU. HOW DO YOU GO ABOUT RESOLVING THESE ISSUES?

It's important when there is a problem like this that you only deal with the people in the room. As difficult as this may seem, you don't want to invoke the name of your parents, what they said, or what you think they want. Try to focus on your opinion and your feelings and the opinion and feelings of your siblings. Make the opinions as much about yourselves as you possibly can. Don't navigate yourself to the middle between your siblings and parents. You will discover that the problem becomes more doable, and from that framework you can resolve the other issues that may exist with your parents. Bonus points if you can actually get the third-party (your parents) in the room with you so they can represent themselves.

11. YOU ARE WORKING ON THESE SKILLS, BEING EMPATHIC, AND PATIENTLY
     TEACHING AND THE OTHER PERSON IS JUST NOT GETTING IT. WHAT CAN YOU
     DO?

First off, good for you you're doing such a good job. Rock on! The main point to make here is that you have to leave room for the other person to understand this stuff on his/her own. I will be duly impressed if you are a master at this by the time you put the book down. For whatever it's worth, I'm still practicing and learning myself. Remember that you chose to take on this project of learning and practicing, and the other person is a bit behind. Be patient. Imagine you are a third grade teacher and little Jimmy is just not getting his multiplication tables. Sure you can yell at him, flunk him, or transfer him somewhere else. The best strategy is to try and come up with another way to help him understand. Don't take it personally that he's not getting it. Certainly look at yourself and if there's anything you need to change about the way you are presenting the information, give it a try. He just might need more time than the other kids. Lastly, remind yourself you don't run the world. There are others forces (including the will and desire of the other person) that can help them in addition to or more than what you are doing.

12.   YOU SCREWED UP BIG TIME. AND THE OTHER PERSON IS UPSET. NOW WHAT?

This would be similar, but not exactly the same, to if you *didn't* screw up and the person was upset. In both cases please convey an empathic understanding of their feelings. If you screwed up, it would be good practice to take responsibility for your behavior. Fix it, change it, and if you don't know how to do either, you should ask. Maybe the other person would have a suggestion.

An apology would certainly be warranted if you felt sorrow. The apology needs to be about you. Don't apologize if the point is to make the other person less upset. In general though it is far more valuable and powerful to be empathic than it is to be apologetic. In the case of you screwing up, the main attention should be on your behavior, not the other person's feelings, (as opposed to if the other person was upset and you didn't do anything wrong).

13. YOU WANT TO CONNECT WITH SOMEONE OF A DIFFERENT CULTURE. OR WE CAN SAY YOU WANT TO GET CLOSER TO SOMEONE YOU DON'T KNOW VERY WELL. WHAT CAN BE THE BATTLE PLAN?

Ask them questions. Listen carefully. What is it like to be them? Try to stall efforts to tell them about yourself. When you throw in attempts to be empathic on top of your inquiries you then create a vicious cycle in the direction of learning more about them and becoming closer. *Empathy does not have to be employed only in intense interpersonal situations or conflicts.* You can actually practice by looking or listening to anybody not even in the room with you. If you saw someone on television you can imagine what you might ask them (don't be shy) if you were with them. What is it like to be that person? Like the guy who just jumped out of an airplane without a parachute and used just a net, or someone who experienced tragedy. The fact that we don't know them personally does not mean we can't use our perceptions and judgments to formulate an empathic response.

14. YOU LIKE YOUR NEIGHBOR, BUT YOUR SPOUSE DOESN'T. CAN'T STAND 'EM. NOW WHAT?

This situation requires structure and boundaries. What are your and what are your spouse's thoughts and feelings. Notice that for both of you the *feelings* about the neighbor (anger, disappointment, joy, pleasure or whatever) are different than your *opinions* about the neighbor, (he or she is nice, mean, a good person, or a bum). Having a conversation with your spouse where you can represent your thoughts or feelings increases the chances you can come up with a social plan that works for the two of you. You also want to try and avoid bringing what the neighbor says or does, or what somebody else says about the neighbor into the conversation as much as possible. That will only complicate the discussion.

For example, you represent yourself in a helpful way by saying, "I think he is a lousy neighbor," or, "I feel uncomfortable around him". Bringing somebody else's thoughts or feelings into the conversation like, "He said we make too much noise," or "his other neighbor doesn't like him either" may tangle the decision process for you and your spouse.

16. YOU ARE SHY, AND YOU ARE GOING TO A PARTY/INTERVIEW/DATE/SO ON. WHAT CAN YOU DO TO PUT YOUR MIND MORE AT EASE?

You can start by reviewing some of the chapter headings of this book. Most all of them will apply in some way or another. Let's touch on them in no particular order. There will be another person or other people there. They will have their own thoughts and feelings (empathize) and will likely be concerned with their own stuff (we try to control our own worlds). Remember that you bring something to the table (all couples are equal) and what actually happens or takes place is ultimately out of your control (G-d runs the world). To help distract you from your own feelings, you can focus on something specific (either the process or content of what is happening), or on the fact that everyone else will be pre-occupied with their own perspective of things (they aren't altruistic; they will say or do what makes sense to them). The pièce de résistance is that you don't know what is going to happen, so whatever negative expectations you may bring to the table are just that—expectations.

16. YOUR FRIEND IS NOT DOING WELL-LET'S SAY HE IS DEPRESSED. YOU WANT TO HELP BUT ARE NOT SURE IF IT'S YOUR PLACE TO ADVISE HIM OR EVEN HOW TO GO ABOUT IT. WHAT CAN YOU DO?

This is a good time to invoke the golden rule again. If you were in that spot, what would you want your friend to do for you? To leave you alone? If so, OK, that is certainly an option. Understand that just being there is a wonderful thing. Conveying empathy would be lovely. The elephant in your brain is the potential advice you want to give. Proceed with caution. You are welcome to load up and fire away with your brilliant counsel and insights, but please recognize that if your friend does not take your advice, that will not be about you. Giving advice that is not well received brings the risk of you taking that personally and creating unneeded distance between you and your hurting friend. If your boundaries are good, fire away with the advice; be prepared to quickly be empathic (not apologetic) if your counsel is not well received.

17.   HOW WOULD THESE SKILLS AND CONCEPTS DIFFER IF THE RELATIONSHIP WAS
      AT WORK, WITH A FRIEND, WITH A FAMILY MEMBER, OR IN A MARRIAGE?

They wouldn't. No matter what the setting, the object would be to try to more clearly delineate what is yours and what is theirs. Conceptualizing the relationship as a covenant lends itself to putting in extra effort because of its permanent nature. Make the goal to work on your own stuff. That is not easy. It is especially hard at first since it will come naturally to see flaws in others before you can find them in yourself.

Remember that game played as a kid with the metal ball resting on two metal sticks? You begin to separate the sticks, and the ball rolls toward you. If you separate them too far, the ball drops out. If you don't separate them enough, the ball just sits there.

It's impossible to describe to someone else how to perform this game successfully. You have to try it yourself and practice. With experience, you will find a balance. For our purposes, with these skills, it's a balance between being empathic with another person versus representing your own thoughts or feelings. Once you have a strategy, vision, or goal of what to work on, try to be patient and kind to yourself. You will become more proficient with practice.

18. YOU READ THIS BOOK AND THINK IT'S ALL FINE AND DANDY HELPING WITH HOW TO DEAL WITH THINGS AS THEY COME UP. BUT HOW CAN YOU DEAL WITH THINGS THAT ARE ALREADY THERE? LET'S SAY YOU HAVE OLD HURT FEELINGS OR EMOTIONAL BAGGAGE YOU CARRY AROUND. HOW CAN YOU LET STUFF GO?

Think of the baggage as just that—baggage. You want to set it down or leave it behind. If you can't do that, at least get some help carrying it. It would therefore help if someone else knew about your baggage. If another person did, there is the hopeful thought that he or she would be empathic toward you. You increase the chances of this happening by sharing your baggage (feelings) with someone else. You help your own cause by advertising it as exactly that. "I am carrying around a lot of baggage right now. Can I unload some of it?" That is a great hint for someone to be empathic with you. If you don't find him or her capable of this, give the person your copy of this book, wait three hours, and try again. In the meantime, while you are waiting, please give yourself the consolation that there is no such thing as an abnormal feeling. There is a reason for your feeling, and there is a way to understand its origin. Achieving this insight will help your own tolerance of your baggage while you wait for help.

CONCLUSION

ONE OF THE greatest Jewish sages was Rabbi Akiva, who lost twenty-four thousand of his students to a plague. The Talmud relates that the students died because they did not treat each other with respect. They were critical of each other, apparently wanting each other to follow the teachings of the Torah to such a degree that their rebukes of each other took on a hypercritical tone. Ideally, they would have been able to maintain their passion for each other's personal accomplishments in Torah study without taking each other's behaviors personally.

Much of what I have shared has been about clarifying interpersonal boundaries and trying to help you see in different ways how you are separate from others. What should come with this separateness is emotional clarity and a better environment to solve problems between people in relationships. Consistent with this is an improved ability to not take things personally. If it belongs to the other person, it is not yours. Somewhat paradoxically, the thought I want to leave you with has to do with how important it is that we are integrally connected to each other.

By our nature, we are gregarious. The success of our community, family, and interpersonal relationships are dependent on how close and connected we are. Integral to developing these connections is how and what we prioritize. Several years ago, I was talking to a dear friend and colleague, and we decided we should get together more often. My not being sure when we could do it was met with his stark comment: "We have to schedule it." Well, we did, and we have been having lunch together every other Wednesday since then. This reminds me of a recent patient encounter where he explained that his not attending an AA meeting was because work was so busy and that he had played golf since "it had been so long since I played." OK by me—no problem. But if you want something to happen, like going to an AA meeting, being consistent with diet or exercise, or improving your relationships, it needs to move up the priority list.

I hope I have given food for thought as to how to fix problems that may arise, but the goal should be to reconnect and stay connected. For Rabbi Akiva's students, their mistake was focusing on their *own* conclusions of what would be best for their fellow man. The proper mind-set would be that each of us has unique gifts, skills, or traits. By keeping track of and being responsible for our own thoughts, feelings, and behavior, we are better able to then blend our features with the strengths and weaknesses of others. Relationships with this type of foundation are what make for a covenant that is durable, healthy, and prosperous.

ABOUT THE AUTHOR

Dr. FINE EARNED his medical degree from The George Washington University in 1986 and completed his residency at the University of Colorado in 1990. Since finishing his formal training in psychiatry, he has treated patients from 5 to 95 years old utilizing individual, couples and family therapy in his own full-time private practice. He has lectured to both medical and non-medical audiences on psychotherapy and psychopharmacology, supervised the work of Marriage and Family Therapist interns and published numerous articles about mental health and health care issues. He rides his bike, davens, and lives with his wife, dogs and cats in Vacaville, California.

Keytothecovenant.com

Made in the USA
Lexington, KY
21 November 2019